The B-29s are Coming

The B-29s are Coming

A Seven-Year-Old Girl in WWII

SETSUKO UKUDA

BOOKLOGIX®
Alpharetta, GA

The author has tried to recreate events, locations, and conversations from his/her memories of them. The author has made every effort to give credit to the source of any images, quotes, or other material contained within and obtain permissions when feasible.

Copyright © 2025 by Setsuko Ukuda

All rights reserved. No part of this book may be reproduced or transmitted in any form or by any means, electronic or mechanical, including photocopying, recording, or any information storage and retrieval system, without permission in writing from the author.

ISBN: 978-1-6653-0888-5

This ISBN is the property of BookLogix for the express purpose of sales and distribution of this title. The content of this book is the property of the copyright holder only. BookLogix does not hold any ownership of the content of this book and is not liable in any way for the materials contained within. The views and opinions expressed in this book are the property of the Author/Copyright holder, and do not necessarily reflect those of BookLogix.

Printed in the United States of America

⊚This paper meets the requirements of ANSI/NISO Z39.48-1992 (Permanence of Paper)

Cover art: Tim Glover
Credit for photographs: Zensho Ukuda, Okinawa Prefecture (Brother of author).

1 0 0 6 2 5

*I wish to dedicate this book to the people of Okinawa. To those who were caught in the middle of the war who suffered and died. May the world never see the likes of this tragedy ever again.
I also wish to dedicate this book to the Ukuda family, my grandchildren and their families, for they are the reason I wrote this.
Finally, to Alex Taylor and Johnny Vardeman for their support and direction in every area of this book.*

CONTENTS

Foreword   ix

Chapter One   *Gentle Island Rhythm*   1

Chapter Two   *Fleeting Peace*   21

Chapter Three   *Winds of War ~*
                               "Typhoon of Steele"   25

Chapter Four   *Shifting Sands*   45

Chapter Five   *An Unbreakable Spirit*
                               and New Era   53

FOREWORD

During World War II, everybody in Okinawa, including children, knew the sight and sound of the B-29. This American bomber actually ended World War II.

Life is so unpredictable. One moment we are having a wonderful, peaceful, and happy life, and the next moment we are living a nightmare. I am constantly looking to the skies for flights of the B-29s. I lose my flip-flops somewhere in the mud and my feet are hurting. We travel to different caves and horse-barns and I'm so tired and hungry, but I'm not supposed to cry.

It is June 1945, and I'm seven years old. Our family, led by my father, fled to Mabuni, which is the southern part of Okinawa. We've been hiding in caves for two months. We are surrounded by the

Setsuko Ukuda

ominous sounds of the B-29 Superfortress's machine guns and whistle bombs. Every minute feels like it is our last, our time to die. This is my story.

Chapter One
Gentle Island Rhythm

IN THE YEAR 1938, I was born on a tiny island called Okinawa. Okinawa is one of many tropical islands in the South Pacific, a little south of mainland Japan, eight hundred miles south of Tokyo. The longest part of Okinawa is less than seventy miles long and the widest part is around seven miles across.

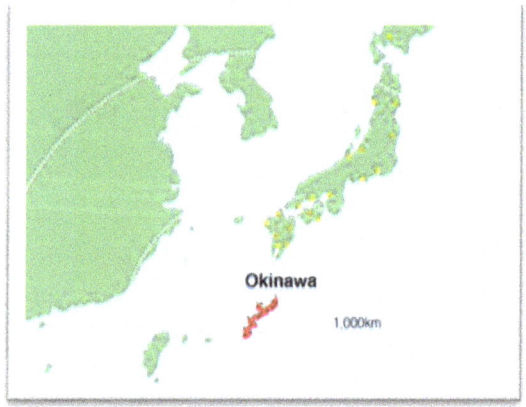

The B-29s are Coming

My father, Zensei, was a farmer—a fairly successful one at that. He was a dedicated, serious, and quiet man. He often gathered all of us together to talk about our great ancestors, reminding us that we should strive every day to live our lives in a way that would make them proud. He told us he had many wishes for us, like our happiness, and the importance of taking our education seriously. Most importantly, he wished for us to be honest, hard-working, good people, who always strove to do the right thing.

One rainy day, my father attended a farmer's meeting and took his brand-new umbrella with him. He was the last to leave the meeting and saw his new umbrella was gone, and only one very old umbrella was left. My mother, Kamado, was upset with him when he got home because she had just purchased the umbrella the day before, and she felt he hadn't been responsible with it.

My father replied, "Why are you mad at me? You should be upset if I left home with an old umbrella and came home with someone else's new umbrella." My father not only spoke to us about life and how we *should* live, but showed us in the way he lived. I have always been honored to be his daughter and a member of the Ukuda family.

In 1669, Makatu, a daughter from the Ukuda family who was written about as being exquisitely beautiful, married an Okinawan king—King Shotei of the Sho family—and became queen.

OKINAWAN KING AND QUEEN TRADITIONAL ROBES

The B-29s are Coming

The king loved poetry. He often wrote poetry and enjoyed playing a game in which he would write the first half of a poem and then ask his subjects to write the ending. Whoever wrote the best ending to the poem was the winner!

The Ukuda family has two tombs in Okinawa that are side-by-side; one for the king and queen, and the other, for the rest of the Ukuda family, is a really big tomb with a high ceiling and an interior that goes a long way back. These tombs are on a hilltop between Shuri Castle and Yonabaru on the east coast.

US SOLDIERS DISCOVERY OF THE
TOMB DURING THE BATTLE OF OKINAWA

The inside of the Ukuda family's tomb has shelves lining the walls for the urns that carry their ashes. Also inside the tomb were three Ukuda family swords, which were a gift from the king to the queen's father. Just before the war found its way to Okinawa, the swords were safely retrieved by an Ukuda family member and were taken to Osaka, Japan, to prevent them from being destroyed by the war. Most recently, the Ukuda family felt it was time for these historic artifacts to be added to the rich cultural past of Okinawa. So as of March 2023, these swords are on display at the Okinawan Prefectural Museum in Naha City.

PHOTO COURTESY OF ZENSHO UKUDA

Setsuko Ukuda

The written Ukuda family tree goes back to the 1500s.

ORIGINAL UKUDA FAMILY TREE BOOK FROM 1500S.

NEW UKUDA FAMILY TREE BOOK WITH ADDITIONS TO THE MID-2000S.

Our ancestors are samurai. Five hundred years ago, Samurai were much different from the more recent samurai of 150 years ago. Rather, they were nobles and had magnificent character and valor. Back then, both Japanese and Okinawan societies were very class-oriented, and the Ukuda family was in the "samurai class." In the 1500s, the families decided who married whom. This is how an Ukuda family member married the king and became queen.

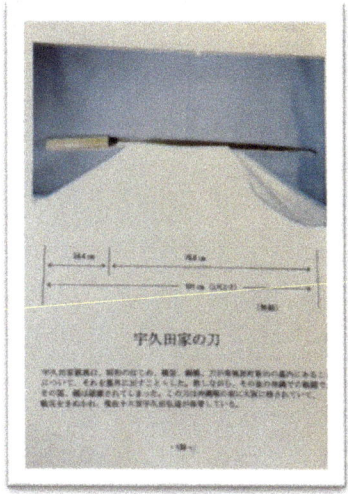

UKUDA
SAMURAI SWORD

Setsuko Ukuda

UKUDA
FAMILY CREST

The B-29s are Coming

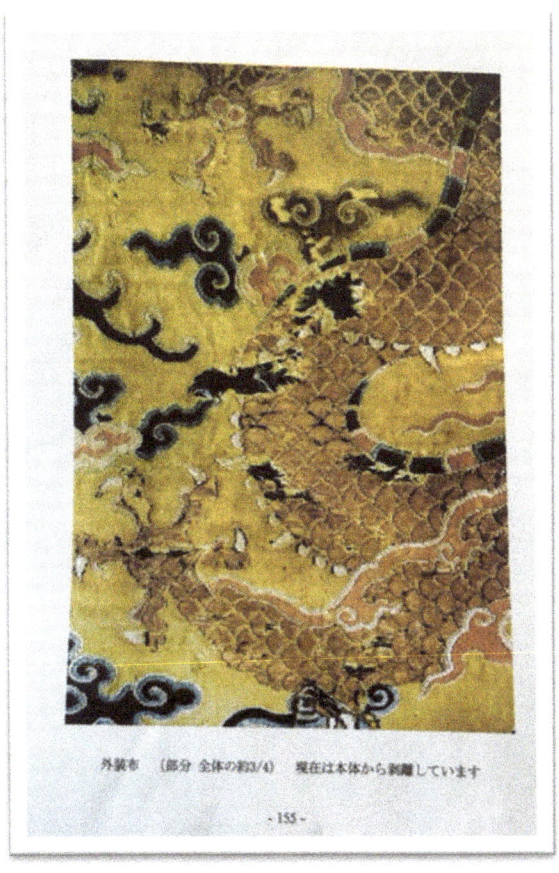

外装布　(部分 全体の約3/4)　現在は本体から剥離しています

- 155 -

UKUDA FAMILY SILK

Setsuko Ukuda

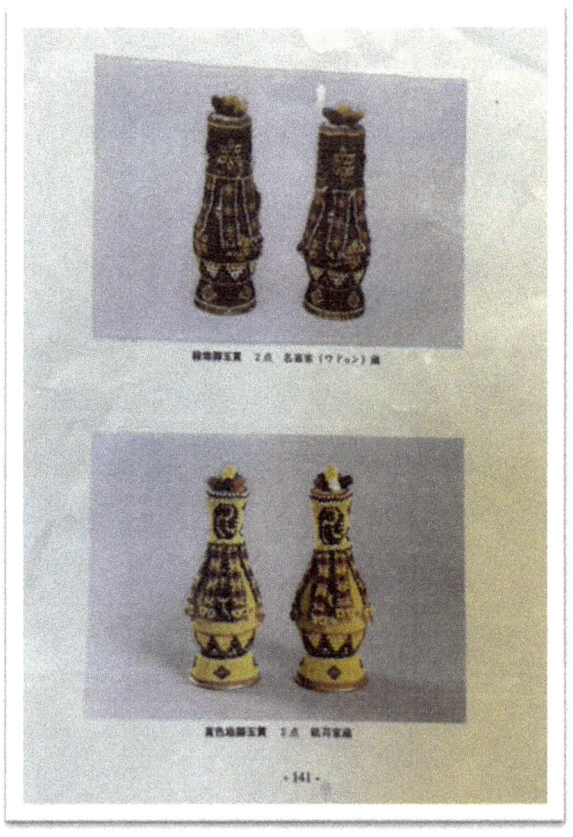

UKUDA FAMILY VASES

The B-29s are Coming

My mother, Kamado, was a free-spirited, stylish woman who always made herself look nice. She was strong, confident, and compassionate. My parents married when they were fifteen years old, as was the custom at the time. Within one year, they had their first baby.

As some mornings go in households with new babies, my mother was in the kitchen one morning and the baby was crying. My father behaved consistent with the late-1800s Japanese male mentality, and did not get up to help. My mother told him she would not live her life without help from her husband, so she took the baby and went back home to her parents. One week later, my father came to apologize and said it would never happen again and, according to my older sister, they were the best of friends and each other's biggest life-long supporters after that.

People who lived at the turn of the century often had large families. I had seven siblings growing up ... seven very noisy siblings—but we were a very happy family. The older I got, the happier I was to have a large family. I have a younger brother, but I was the youngest daughter in the family, and as they say in the US, I was a "daddy's girl."

But all families often suffer sadness, and mine came on December 14, 1993, when at age ninety-six, my mother passed away. She must have had really good genes because even at ninety-six, she slept on a tatami floor mat and could stand up without grabbing onto anything to help her. She only suffered from cataracts and minor arthritis in her left knee. Otherwise, she led an adventurous life and gave credit to her husband, saying, "Your father is gone, but he's still watching over me." Some of her adventures included trips to different places around mainland Japan with her senior citizens group, and dancing with another senior citizen dance group. She wasn't only physically energetic; she was also very sharp mentally. She didn't miss a thing! She was like an Indian Chief, strong and wise.

I was very sad when she passed away. I could no longer see or talk to her, but I knew she had a fully lived life. She was surrounded by her children and grandchildren, who loved and cherished her, and I'm happy for this. I miss her more now than before. Next time I see my mother, I will give her a big hug and never let her go.

I grew up climbing trees and rocks and running around wide-open fields. I would spend lazy days lying in fields surrounded by daisy-like flowers everywhere. My friends and I watched the clouds form different shapes and we would play guessing games as the shapes formed. It filled our days with laughter. We walked along rocky riverbanks and when we were lucky, we found wild, delicious, yummy grapes! It was like we were in a chapter of the American television show, *Little House on the Prairie.*

Setsuko Ukuda

MY HOMETOWN STREET WHERE I GREW UP

The B-29s are Coming

Setsuko Ukuda

PHOTOS COURTESY OF ZENSHO UKUDA

Each year, in the month of September, when these pompous flowers bloomed, it was a sign that fall had arrived. I have wonderful memories of my youth . . . fun, happy, and carefree memories—really, they were the best years of my life.

Where we grew up was just like a Norman Rockwell-style village, where kids wore their Panama hats and walked barefoot with their dogs along dusty trails. It was so peaceful and such a wholesome scene. I remember after an overnight rain carried into the morning, we rushed up the mountain to pick huge, plump mushrooms that grew around all of the old trees after a good rain. My mother cooked the mushrooms with vegetables, and our own chickens, sautéing them into a scrumptious meal. These peaceful and fun days continued during the start of the war. Not much changed.

Chapter Two

Fleeting Peace

BEFORE THE BATTLE BECAME heavy, there were many Japanese soldiers stationed nearby, coming in and out of our home. They were very friendly and fun-loving men. A few in particular loved to play Japanese Go (a Chess-type of game) with my father. But my father was too good at the game, and no matter how hard they tried, they could never beat him. These fun times filled our home with a lot of laughter.

I was six years old in April 1945, and the war was getting closer every day, so my father went out searching for a place of safety for our family. Half a mile from our home, he dug to reveal a cave large enough for all eight of us to fit safely and comfortably. For me and my brothers and sisters, it was another adventure since we were going to stay in the caves like a camping trip. Japanese soldiers also dug caves surrounding ours. These caves actually connected to each other deep in the trenches. It was a good thing the caves were connected, because we had a lot of fun with each other and with the soldiers, playing games there.

I, like other children, and my brothers and sisters looked forward to playing in and around the cave and even going deep inside the trenches of the cave to play. The soldiers created a fun, adventurous environment for us. They let us use their binoculars to see the nearby city of Naha and told us stories and the history of our land. One of the officers was very close to our family. His name was Lieutenant Iwasaki. He worked during the day as a communications officer. At night, we all gathered around him as he sang songs and played his guitar. I remember how beautiful his voice was. But sometimes, his voice was sad and I cried. It was almost like a prediction which foretold the future. I was unaware that the war would change from what it was. I believed we could play in the caves as the war happened around us.

Within two weeks, the war escalated and our family needed to relocate to a safer place. My memory recalls "all hell broke loose!" My father decided to move us to the southern part of Okinawa, but Lieutenant Iwasaki said it would be the most dangerous place. Because of the briefings Lieutenant Iwasaki attended, he knew the likelihood of American landings on the southern end of the island was high. However, my father grew up in the southern part of the island, so he was familiar with the many deep caves there and felt it was safer for us. Regardless of Lieutenant Iwasaki's warning, my father's mind was made up, and we prepared to move to the south. As we prepared to embark on our long, perilous journey, we were unaware the decision he made would prove to be fatal.

The day we left Shuri, Lieutenant Iwasaki gave me a gift. It was actually a gift for his wife, but he decided to give it to me as a parting gift. It was the most beautiful, deep-red lacquer jewelry box any of us had ever seen. We all hugged and parted ways as Lieutenant Iwasaki remained at his post. After the war, we found out he had been asking around about our family. We were so happy he had survived, but because of the post-war chaos, we never got to see him again. He was truly an unforgettable man.

Chapter Three

Winds of War ~ "Typhoon of Steele"

AS WE EMBARKED ON our long, perilous journey south to our destination, Mabuni, we saw formations of B-29 bombers in the sky throughout the day, every day. Along the way, we stopped to sleep in farmers' barns and caves. It was the rainy season, so it made our trek slower and more difficult. There was no talking while we walked, only the sound of our feet in the mud. I only had flip-flops on and quickly lost those in the mud right at the beginning of our journey, so for the rest of the trip, I had to walk barefoot.

Along the way, we met all different Okinawan people and soldiers. One family told us Japanese soldiers took their cave and that they had no place to go. Some soldiers were good, but others were bad.

The good soldiers were kind and caring. They showed empathy for the Okinawan people caught in the middle. They would come back and tell my father and other families which avenues were safe and which led to danger.

The bad soldiers were ruthless and had a total disregard for the well-being of the Okinawan people, using them only for resources before moving on.

As we rested in our cave, nearly all the way to Mabuni, two soldiers picked my father and my sixteen-year-old sister, Yoshiko, to be part of a ten-person crew to carry large bags of rice back to Shuri, our home, with the Shuri line just north of the town. Shuri Castle is located in Shuri, Okinawa Prefecture, which is just south of an imaginary line if you were to cut Okinawa in half. The castle was in use during the Sanzan period in the early 1300s. Between 1429 and 1879, it was the palace of the Ryukyu Kingdom, and in 1945, it was almost completely destroyed during the Battle of Okinawa.

Once the rice was delivered to Shuri, the soldiers there would, in return, give rice to each person. My family was frightened by this because my father and sister were ordered to walk back through the area we had just passed through, which was now considered a war zone. Bombs were exploding on the land every moment of the day and night. My mother was almost certain my father and Yoshiko would not return. With no choice but to do as they were ordered, my father, sister, and eight others started back to Shuri with bags of rice over their shoulders. All we could do was wait.

The group of ten kept moving and stayed together. They did not stop during the day, or rest at night for fear they would be killed by the bombing. Sure enough, on that first and only night carrying the rice, bombs exploded all around them, killing many of the ten people in the group. One could only imagine what they were thinking and feeling. Were they using the light from the bomb blasts that lit up the countryside to look for each other in hopes their loved ones were still alive? Or were they ducking their heads in complete fear? What a nightmare! Just unimaginable!

My father, yelling out into the darkness in between the light of the bomb blasts, unable to see anything, shouted Yoshiko's name. He waited and waited for her to yell back, and finally, she replied, "I'm okay!" There was nothing they could do but keep moving. Because they didn't stop, it took them just one night to reach Shuri. When they delivered the bags of rice, the remaining people in the group couldn't believe that in return, all they were given was a handful of rice. My father was furious. We thought it was cruel and disingenuous, but this is how the Japanese treated Okinawan people, even though we are the same citizens of Japan.

Those who remained began to walk back to their families waiting for them where they were chosen to carry the rice. Thankfully, my father and sister made it back to us safely. Yoshiko was so sick when she returned, she didn't eat at all and slept for three days, suffering from mental and physical exhaustion along with a high fever. After she felt better, my family finally picked up and continued to Mabuni.

When we arrived, there were no caves left, only a big rock. The top of the rock was large enough for us to hide under, but the front and both sides were wide open. We had hoped it was only temporary, but in the following days, we came to realize there was just nothing left.

Setsuko Ukuda

The B-29s are Coming

Setsuko Ukuda

ZENSHO UKUDA SHOWING HIS
PHOTOGRAPHY OF THE CAVES AT MABUNI

In the safety of the surrounding caves, they had the freedom to go deep within to sit, stand, and talk without drawing attention to themselves or being in the line of fire. However, our family did not have that luxury, since cover was only offered from the rock overhead. Because of constant flying objects and fire, we were told to be silent and lie down close together all day and night long. It was torture for me and my siblings, who just had too much energy. We felt like sardines in a can. No one brought a book or any toys, we only carried little food and survival items, such as first-aid supplies, toilet tissue, and pots and pans. The only clothes we brought with us were what we wore when we started our journey. It was a long, scary, and awful twenty-four hours in Mabuni. One day seemed like a lifetime. Bombs, machine guns, and B-29s were everywhere, never ceasing. The ominous sound of B-29s is unforgettable—the horror of war was upon us.

One afternoon, two Japanese soldiers—one high-ranking and the other low-ranking—came to my father. "Use these grenades," the high-ranking officer said, "to protect your family when the Americans come." We understood what they meant. The soldiers expected my father to kill himself and us before the Americans had the chance to. Once the two soldiers quickly left, my father said, "If the Americans kill us, there is nothing we can do about it. But we will not take our own lives!"

The next morning, the lower-ranking officer returned discretely and told Father, "The Americans aren't going to kill civilians, so don't do it!" Then he quickly disappeared.

The Japanese military must have indoctrinated the soldiers to be ruthless and relentless in order to be good soldiers. Those who proved to be ruthless and relentless were often quickly promoted all the way to the top. Those who were not didn't have a choice but to follow orders. The soldier who returned to tell us not to use the grenade risked his life to tell my father the truth. Without a doubt, he was a kind and courageous man and we hope he made it through the war safely to return to his family.

Our typical day of survival, meal-wise, consisted of one meal per day. My mother made very watery miso soup, with cabbage, carrots, and potatoes. There was a farm nearby, and the farmer's family was hiding in one of the caves, so it was easy for us to "borrow" their vegetables for our soup. There was also a single well, and it was the only source of water in the area, but it was far away in a wide-open area. Bombs reigning down made the trek to the well very dangerous, but my father went every day. Water was only for drinking since it was so scarce.

One day, my father went out for food and came back wearing a Japanese soldier's uniform. When we asked what happened, my father said a Japanese soldier wanted to switch clothes with him, so he would look like a civilian while my father, wearing a Japanese uniform, would be a target for the American soldiers. You see, the Japanese military was hyperfocused on winning the war, at the expense of their humanity.

There were Japanese communication soldiers in a cave about forty feet away from our rock. We could hear them using Morse code frequently. Their cave was shaped like a *V*, tilted sideways. We saw them slide in and climb out all the time. One awful, clear, windless day, the Americans dropped a huge drum can right in front of their cave. When the drum can hit the ground, liquid chemicals and gasses spilled into their cave. What we heard and witnessed next was complete horror. There were monstrous, other-worldly screams as the Japanese soldiers ran out of their cave. In an instant, the skin all over their bodies was peeled off and hanging from their bones. Their faces were swollen to twice their normal size, and their eyes bulged from their sockets. We looked at them and froze. We were speechless, not knowing what to do for these men. They died almost instantly.

Reflecting back, I'm surprised we didn't lose our minds after witnessing this. It was a sight and sound no human mind could ever erase. After that, all I could think of was how close the soldiers' cave was to ours. If the drum can was even the slightest degree off, we would have been consumed as well.

Father said, "The Americans must have picked up their signal and pinpoint dropped it right on their cave to halt communications." Really, it was a miracle we survived so many instances like this.

There was a piece of a torn parachute in the tall trees on top of a hill we used to gauge wind speed. If the parachute was swaying, we knew it was a windy day. When the parachute was not moving, we knew it could be deadly for us if gas-bombing runs occurred. Yoshiko, gave us each wet washcloths to place over our noses and mouths to protect us from the gas bombs.

The morning of June 21, 1945, was a usual morning waking up to the sound of bombs and guns. Every day brought with it intense, mental torture. I was lying on my back and my father was next to me, lying sideways with his arm supporting his head. Suddenly, a piece of burning metal came from my right side. It passed right over me and hit my father in his stomach. He died instantly and his internal organs spilled next to my left arm. Everyone was stunned and horrified. Speechless. We were silent for a long time, and then my sister,

Mitsuko, finally cried out, "I wish it were me instead of Father!"

My mother ran to comfort her and told her not to speak that way. At the same time, my other older sister, Yoshiko, ran over to Father, scooped up his internal organs, and tried to put them back into his body in hopes he would be okay if everything were in place. We were all in complete shock, unsure what to do. Then, we all just cried and cried. It was a horrible nightmare. That day, our world ended.

Two days later, we heard a PA system on a US Navy ship telling us in Japanese, "The war is over! Come out!" The man speaking was a second-generation Japanese (nisei). We dropped everything and went outside. It was a long hill to climb, but we put our hands up and saw Americans standing on top of the hill. When we reached the very top of the hill, we saw Americans up close for the very first time. They were giants! Looking at them was just like looking at the sky! I still remember the first time I saw the Americans, I thought, *Wow!*

They have blue eyes and blond hair! They look like Martians! I had seen blue-eyed goats before, but never a blue-eyed human.

The Americans were very nice and gentle. They gave us chewing gum and then motioned with their hands to move over and sit down between two large rocks. We heard gunfire and knew it was coming from the Japanese soldiers. The Japanese soldiers were shooting 7.7 deadly rifles! The American soldiers moved us between the rocks so we wouldn't get hit by cross-fire. We didn't know why the war was over, but the Japanese were still shooting as if it wasn't. We felt safe though, because the American soldiers were there to protect us. This was all completely different from what that high-ranking Japanese soldier had once told my father.

Throughout the war, the Japanese soldiers were unpredictable. We didn't know who was good and who was bad, but we were more afraid of the Japanese soldiers than the American soldiers.

As we were taking cover inside the cave, a bomb exploded nearby and fiery shrapnel went flying in every direction. A piece of shrapnel landed on my head and cheek. Everyone immediately jumped on my head to put out the fire. Within a few days, the war would be over, and directly after it ended, American medics took care of the burn on my cheek Though the scar on my cheek is still visible, I consider it my war memento.

Another story relating to the aid rendered to Okinawans by the American soldiers was documented and later turned up in newspaper articles. The story published in an Okinawan newspaper chronicled an American medic who had found a wounded six-year-old boy lying in the middle of a field. The medic discovered that he was still alive and began providing care for the little boy. Suddenly, the medic noticed two Japanese soldiers standing behind him with their rifles. The Japanese soldiers saw that the American medic was helping the little boy giving him first aid, so they turned and walked away. The medic took the boy to an American hospital and saved his life. Forty-two years after the war, this American medic came back to Okinawa with his wife, looking for the little boy he had saved during the war. The medic used the newspaper clipping to look for the little boy, anticipating seeing him again. After a long search, they finally found each other. The medic and his wife did not have any children, so even though the boy he saved was now a grown man, they were hoping to bring him back to the US and make him part of their family. Since this Okinawan boy was now in his mid-forties and had a family of his own, of course this was not possible but a nice gesture.

Setsuko Ukuda

COURTESY OF *LIFE* MAGAZINE: THIS PHOTO SUMS UP HOW WE FELT ABOUT THE AMERICAN SOLDIERS WITH THEIR KIND HEARTS, AS THEY NURSED A BABY GOAT BACK TO HEALTH.

The B-29s are Coming

On their way back to the US, the medic and his wife stopped for a few days in Tokyo. He used the newspaper clipping to begin searching for the two Japanese soldiers he encountered in Okinawa during the war. Eventually, they found each other and became friends. The medic and his wife returned home to the US, and it was a happy ending!

When it was safe to move from the top of the hill, the American soldiers took us to northern Okinawa on a Naval ship. We had to move north because so many people died in the small area, and the air and ground were extremely polluted. For example, we heard that one of our fellow Okinawans who was traveling with us had stepped in a dead soldier's stomach. The pollution was horrid. What was a seven-year-old girl to do with all the noise, death, and destruction? Those who have never experienced war could never believe the horrible and unimaginable smell of decaying bodies. It's a smell you remember and carry with you for the rest of your life!

Chapter Four
Shifting Sands

WE LIVED IN NORTHERN Okinawa for about a year and a half. We liked it there. It was right next to the ocean and we played there all day long. On windy days, big waves pushed seaweed on shore, and my mother made soup with the seaweed. Occasionally, we received canned food, like canned beef and saltine crackers. Of course, this was not nearly enough, and we were hungry all the time. We were still very thankful because, thank God, we were not having to hide and live in the rocks and caves anymore.

During this time, several adults expressed concern that we were not learning as it was not good for kids to go so long without school lessons. Right away, they gathered six to seven kids and, despite not having pencils or paper, gave us lessons in math and reading. One big rock by the ocean was our chair. Sitting on this rock as we learned was so fun, occasionally getting splashed on our backs by the waves. We called this the "blue sky classroom."

The B-29s are Coming

Setsuko Ukuda

Within one month, we were learning in a real school classroom. This school was completely intact from the war. It was a beautiful, big wooden school with shiny wooden columns and floors. The school was three miles from home and there were a lot of students. Even though it was a long walk, we had fun on our journey because of the beautiful scenery. There were tall mountains on the left, a beautiful ocean on the right, and Japanese pine trees, like bonsai trees, that lined our route. The road was winding all the way to the school.

Every day, when school was over, our teacher gave us a huge Butterfinger candy bar. I guess they wanted to encourage us to return to school each day! Did you know that during the 1940s, candy bars were almost twice the size of today's candy bars? They were huge! It was quite a handful for a seven-year-old! On the way home, we munched on our candy bars and sang our favorite songs, taking in the beautiful scenery. It was a blissful time. Even during the start of the recovery from war, we kids were blessed. We could find fun, happiness, and lots of laughter in the little things.

I had fun during the day, but nights were very sad and lonely. Especially just before the sun set, I cried uncontrollably because my father was my sun in the sky, and I had felt—as the sun set—he was leaving us, never able to return. The whole family missed him, but I was "daddy's girl." I cried myself to sleep for a long time and I still miss him very much, forever and ever. He worked so hard every day for us, and I am sad and hurt he died before he had a chance to enjoy his life. I am so sorry, my dear father. I love you so much.

We struggled and were hungry all the time, but we had fun—except for my poor mother. It must have been so hard for her to care for us all by herself. We didn't know anything about her agony and struggle, but today we understand what she went through.

A year and a half later, we were moved back to Shuri. There, we lived for six months in a huge tent with six other families. Our next move was back to our original home and we started going to school in Shuri. We went to school for half the day, and spent the other half working to fill bomb holes. There were a few trees and so many bomb holes everywhere; it was a mess beyond belief. After we leveled the ground, a grass bungalow-style classroom was built to keep us dry during the rain and protect us from the strong, steamy Okinawan sun. A beautiful new wooden classroom was built for us six months later and we had to take our shoes off when we entered.

As soon as we arrived for school in the morning, they would give us tiny red-colored one-a-day type vitamins and boiled water in a large pan, adding powdered milk, for us to drink for our nourishment. Life was a challenging task, but slowly, we were moving in the right direction. The momentum of the Okinawan people may have been slowed down because of the war, but it could never be stopped. It is a "do or die" strategy and because of that, life was steadily improving.

I cannot continue my story without mentioning a great Japanese Navy Vice Admiral named Miroru Oota. He was stationed in Okinawa during the war, and he was a noble and righteous man. He understood that the Okinawan people suffered tremendously. He telegrammed the Japanese government, pleading with them to repair the war-torn island of Okinawa, as he saw first-hand how the citizens were caught in the middle of the battle, betrayed by the Japanese, and as a result, killed so brutally. Sadly, Vice Admiral Oota took his own life after sending this telegram.

HQ PICTURE

Chapter Five

An Unbreakable Spirit and New Era

ALONG WITH THE EARLIER story about my father being ordered to trade clothes with a Japanese soldier, there's also an account of my friend Kyoko and her four-year-old brother. They were playing with a ball in the front yard when the ball rolled into the street and in front of a Japanese soldier on horseback. The soldier jumped off his horse, drew his sword, and yelled at the little boy. Their father begged the Japanese soldier not to hurt his son, but the Japanese soldiers could be cruel and ruthless.

Ten years after the war, I was starting high school, and my older twin sisters, Mitsuko and Yoneko, had just graduated. After my sisters graduated, their teacher came to see my mother to ask her about sending them to college, since they were straight-A students. Unfortunately, it wasn't possible. My mother couldn't afford college and needed every helping hand she could get.

I had been taking gymnastics and made the school competitive team my freshman year.

I participated in all events, including the balance beam and floor exercise. Our school team won first place every year. No other school could compete with our team. My coach suggested I attend college in mainland Japan and one day return to Okinawa to become a PE teacher at Shuri High School. I knew that wouldn't be possible, but I told her I would think about it. The truth is, I did not want to be a PE teacher for two reasons:

1) In 1956, we didn't have a gym, so PE was held outside in the hot sun. Okinawa is a tropical island and naturally, there are more warmer, direct sun days, so we all are naturally tan and darker than mainland Japanese people.
2) Traditionally, PE teachers' hair are always chopped short and this PE teacher was no exception. Her skin was so dark that when she smiled, her teeth were bright white and just jumped out at you!

It was a good thing she was attractive without makeup. I, however, was the complete opposite. I like makeup and high heels.

After graduating high school, I went to the Air Force base employment office, took an English test, and passed. (You passed the test if you got at least a 75 percent or higher.) The office sent me to Naha

Base Exchange (BX), which was the store for military personnel and their families. The BX was the perfect job for me, and I had a great time working there.

The overseas BX was huge, like a department store. If you were looking for a husband, this was the best place to be; you could pick and choose too! I worked in the cosmetics department, so I had a few American housewife friends. When their husbands went off to TDY (Temporary Duty Assignment) for several weeks at a time, they asked me to stay with them, even though they lived on the base. It was a great opportunity to use my English skills and learn about American culture.

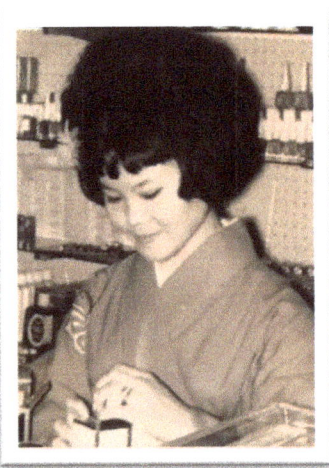

One of my friends was called Martha. I would

go to her home after work and then go straight to work the next day. I had a great time and felt it was also a productive experience. They had a four-year-old son named Marty and I practiced my English with him. Martha was a great friend. She often made my favorite meal, spaghetti. Other times, meatloaf was cooking when I arrived at her house. I can still remember it as a wonderful memory.

Around this same time, my younger brother, Zensho, graduated from high school. Our financial situation was a little better, so this made it possible for him to attend college! He was the only one in my family to do so. He attended the prestigious University of the Ryukyus in Okinawa—one of the most reputable universities in Japan.

My sweetest memories of my family and life were during the early '60s. Zensho would go to university for classes and then return home for dinner. Every night after dinner, we would all pile in front of the television, just like that scene in Disney's *101 Dalmatians*. Our favorite programs to watch were *Raw Hide*, *Dr. Ben Casey*, *Dr. Kildare*, *Bat*

Masterson, etc. It seemed like Clint Eastwood and all of the other characters in these shows could speak perfect Japanese, because even their dubbed-over voices sounded just like Clint and the other actors. It was the highlight of our day. We were together and happy.

Classical music was playing in our home all the time because my sister Yoneko was a huge fan. I heard it every day and unconsciously memorized those pieces—I found myself humming along to them. I'm glad she influenced me to love classical music. Many times, I wish these moments would never change and could go on, just us, together forever. Those are my nostalgic memories.

In 1963, I met my now-ex-husband at the BX. He was tall, handsome, and had blue eyes. Yes, I had married one of the Martians! We came to the US in 1967. Every two years, we moved to a different state, which I loved. Upon arrival to the US, our first station was MacDill AFB in the Tampa area. The next rotation was England AFB in Alexandria, Louisiana. Our third rotation was Eglin AFB in Fort Walton Beach, Florida.

We saw and experienced a lot of places. My favorite station would probably be Eglin AFB in Fort Walton Beach. There, I met my best friend to this day, Nancy. We were not at other two stations long enough to make many friends.

My Martian husband decided to go back to college and finish his degree in 1974, which he did. He was in the US Army Reserves and was also a very successful healthcare consultant.

In early 1991, I was going through another agonizing time in my life. This time, it was over my marriage. Both my daughters, Donna and Cara, helped me in so many ways during this desolate time. One day, at the beginning of the fall of my marriage, I called my older daughter, Donna, at work. She dropped everything she was doing and stayed with me that stifling day. She tried helping both of us just get through a conversation civilly with so much hurt and emotions flowing. She even bought tickets to see Perry Como (one of my favorite music artists) at Atlanta's Fox Theatre for both of us and I loved his performance that night. This was her last attempt to save us from drowning. Thank you, Donna, for your love and support, I love you.

Soon though, our marriage ended, and I was left alone, shocked, angry, and desolate. I felt like I was all by myself in this world and because I was heartbroken, I couldn't eat or sleep. The more I thought about it, the angrier I got. However, I refused to lie down and die. I stood up, steely-eyed, and with all of my divine energy, I moved forward one step at a time. Sometimes, I felt it would have been much easier to just drop dead, but other times I refused to be the victim. That was how my father taught us to live our lives; you fall down ten times, you get up ten times.

On Valentine's Day 1992, my niece Keiko, sent me a long stem chocolate flower rose in a beautiful box. Just when I was at my lowest point in my life, this came at the time I desperately needed such a kind, loving gesture. Thank you, Keiko-Chan, for your sweet heart.

Soon, I found a job teaching Japanese to corporate executives who traveled to Japan for business. I taught Japanese for seven years and loved it. However, when there were no students signed up to learn Japanese, I didn't have a job. One day, my younger daughter, Cara, gave me information that the airport was looking for bilingual employees, and that's how I got a job at Hartsfield-Jackson Atlanta International Airport, in the months leading up to the 1996 Olympic Games. I enjoyed this job and the many people I met there from all over the world. I even met some celebrities like Martin Sheen, Mary of the music group Peter, Paul, and Mary, Marie Osmond, Halle Berry, John Denver (without his guitar!), and Dale Murphy (he asked me where the best place to eat was). I worked there for two and a half years, however, standing nine hours in high heels became too hard on me. I kept my eyes out for something new, which led to later becoming a courier with an Atlanta newspaper.

In November of 2004, I happily retired and am surrounded by my two wonderful daughters, Donna and Cara, and their wonderful families. I have lived with my youngest daughter, Cara, and her husband, Ken, since the mid-1990's. Since then, I have watched over my youngest grandson and granddaughter since they were born, and my daily life has been consumed with them. Now that they are grown, I suddenly feel like an empty-nester.

I have four incredible grandchildren. I made it out of the war alive and through a divorce; this is how I came about writing this memoir. I feel the methodology for my life is correct, and everything has purpose. Through it all, I have been made stronger and wiser, believing in myself and having gained much more than I have lost. My faith is everything. With it, I can accomplish anything. I feel my life is an affirmation of the joy of being alive. I am happy with my life; I am just where I should be right now, and I feel it is a wonderful life!

I wish for my children, grandchildren, and beyond, the same ideals and strategy of life that my father wanted for us. Some say, "A comfortable zone is wonderful, but nothing grows there." I wholeheartedly agree with this quote. We grow because we struggle. Life is a learning journey.

The B-29s are Coming

A light has now shown on my journey into darkness.

Powerful engines of B-29s are no longer roaring overhead. Dancing figures of long-passed family and friends are now quiet.

I am an elderly lady with a wonderful family living in a very special country.

All is well!

MODERN-DAY DOWNTOWN NAHA, OKINAWA

DONNA'S FAMILY

CARA'S FAMILY

The B-29s are Coming

SETSUKO'S MOTHER

Setsuko Ukuda

SETSUKO UKUDA LIVES IN GAINSVILLE, GA.

www.ingramcontent.com/pod-product-compliance
Lightning Source LLC
Chambersburg PA
CBHW061751070526
44585CB00025B/2862